Tennessee's Partner

Loyalty, Tragedy & True Friendship in the Wild American West

A Modern Translation
Adapted for the Contemporary Reader

Bret Harte

Translated by Tim Zengerink

Table of Contents

Preface
Message to the Reader

Rebuilding the Greatest Library in Human History

Thousands of years ago, the Library of Alexandria was the heart of global knowledge — a sanctuary where the wisdom of every known civilization was gathered and shared freely.

And then, it was lost.

Now, we're rebuilding it — and you are invited to join us.

At the Library of Alexandria, we've set out to make every book available to every person on Earth — not just in print, but in every language, every format, and for every reader.

Here's how we do it:

- **Deluxe Print Editions at True Printing Cost** - Order any book as a high-quality paperback, elegant hardcover, or stunning boxset — and only pay what it costs to print. No markups. No middlemen.
- **Unlimited Access to the Greatest Works** - Enjoy thousands of timeless classics — from Plato to Shakespeare to Tolstoy — in beautiful, modern eBook and audiobook editions. Read and listen without limits — for every reader, everywhere.
- **Modern Translations for Every Language & Dialect** - We're reimagining the classics in clear, accessible language — and translating them into every dialect imaginable. Everyone deserves to understand humanity's greatest ideas.

When you visit **LibraryofAlexandria.com**, you're not just accessing books — you're joining a global movement to restore, preserve, and share the wisdom of civilization.

Join us today at LibraryofAlexandria.com

Together, we'll ensure the light of human wisdom never fades again.

With gratitude,

The Modern Library of Alexandria Team

Visit:
www.libraryofalexandria.com
Or scan the code below:

1

Introduction

Friendship Forged in the Frontier

Bret Harte's *Tennessee's Partner* is more than a Western tale of outlaws, rough miners, and frontier justice; it is a timeless exploration of loyalty, sacrifice, and the profound, unspoken bonds of friendship. Written in 1869, the story reflects the harsh realities of the mid-19th-century American West while elevating them into a narrative of emotional depth and moral complexity. Set in a rough mining camp during the California Gold Rush, the story follows two men—Tennessee and his unnamed partner—whose lives are intertwined not just by circumstance but by a deep, enduring loyalty that defies judgment, misunderstanding, and social convention.

The story's opening paints a vivid picture of life in a mining town—dusty streets, raucous saloons, and men hardened by the pursuit of gold and the struggles of frontier existence. Yet, within this rugged environment, Harte introduces a relationship that stands apart. Tennessee, a charming but reckless man, lives a life of indulgence and questionable choices. His partner, on the other hand, is steady, reserved, and unwaveringly loyal. The contrast between these two characters creates a dynamic that speaks to one of Harte's central themes: true friendship is not forged by perfection or shared morality, but by a commitment to stand by someone despite their flaws.

Tennessee's Partner is a story that challenges conventional notions of virtue. The miners in the story may not live by the laws of the civilized East, but they operate within their own moral code—one shaped by hardship, necessity, and a sense of communal respect. Harte captures this ethos beautifully, demonstrating how even in a place often associated with greed and lawlessness, values such as loyalty and compassion still thrive.

As readers, we are drawn into the emotional heart of the story when Tennessee, caught for a crime, faces judgment at the hands of his peers. It is his partner's unwavering loyalty—his refusal to abandon or condemn his friend—that transforms the tale from a simple Western narrative into something universally human. Harte's brilliance lies in his ability to take the rough textures of frontier life and polish them into moments of tenderness and grace that resonate with readers across generations.

Loyalty, Sacrifice, and the Human Heart

The story of Tennessee and his partner is, above all, an ode to unwavering loyalty. The partner is a man of few words, but his actions speak volumes. His steadfastness in the face of Tennessee's shortcomings illustrates a kind of friendship that is increasingly rare: one not based on convenience, personal gain, or moral alignment, but on a deeper, almost instinctual understanding of another person's worth.

When Tennessee faces the ultimate penalty for his crimes, his partner does not attempt to argue his innocence or downplay his mistakes. Instead, he acknowledges Tennessee's humanity, offering both tangible support and silent solidarity. This moment, often cited as one of the most moving scenes in Harte's work, reflects the author's keen understanding of the human heart. Harte suggests that true friendship transcends societal expectations and that the measure of a relationship lies not in perfection but in presence—the willingness to stand by someone when they are most vulnerable.

The tragic ending of the story, where the partner's grief and quiet devotion culminate in his final act of loyalty, elevates *Tennessee's Partner* beyond the confines of a Western tale. It becomes a meditation on the enduring power of love and friendship, even in the face of death. In the stark, unrelenting landscape of the frontier, where life is often brutal and short, these small but profound acts of kindness and loyalty shine all the brighter.

This focus on emotional depth was unusual for Western literature of the time, which often emphasized action, rugged individualism, and survival. Harte, however, was a pioneer in blending local color with universal themes, proving that even the roughest of characters could reveal deep moral truths. His portrayal of Tennessee's partner, in particular, challenges stereotypes of masculinity by showing that strength and tenderness can coexist. The partner's quiet resilience, his refusal to abandon Tennessee, and his ultimate sacrifice remind us that true courage lies not just in facing danger but in standing by the people we love, no matter the cost.

Bret Harte's Influence and Enduring Legacy

Bret Harte was one of the first American writers to bring the stories of the California Gold Rush to a national audience. With his keen observational skills, sharp humor, and deep empathy for his characters, Harte helped to shape the Western literary tradition while elevating it into a form of art that explored universal human emotions. *Tennessee's Partner*, like his other well-known works *(The Luck of Roaring*

Camp, The Outcasts of Poker Flat), combines the gritty realism of frontier life with moments of extraordinary tenderness and moral insight.

Harte's literary style—marked by vivid descriptions, colorful dialogue, and a careful balance of humor and pathos—has influenced countless writers, from Mark Twain to Jack London. What sets him apart, however, is his ability to find humanity in unlikely places. While his stories often depict rough, morally ambiguous characters, Harte shows that these individuals are capable of grace, kindness, and profound emotional connections.

In *Tennessee's Partner*, this ability is on full display. The story reminds us that loyalty and love are not confined to the refined or the civilized; they can flourish even in the most rugged of settings. Harte's miners, gamblers, and outcasts may not conform to traditional social norms, but their humanity is no less real. Through his portrayal of Tennessee and his partner, Harte suggests that the values we hold most dear—loyalty, friendship, sacrifice—are not bound by class, education, or geography. They are, instead, fundamental to the human condition.

Even today, over 150 years after its publication, *Tennessee's Partner* continues to resonate with readers. Its themes are timeless, its characters unforgettable, and its message as relevant as ever. In a world where relationships are often tested by distance, misunderstanding, or adversity, Harte's story stands as a testament to the enduring power of standing by those we love.

For modern readers, the story is also a valuable glimpse into the culture of the Gold Rush era, offering not just entertainment but historical insight. Harte's vivid depictions of camp life, with its mixture of camaraderie, danger, and rough humor, create a rich backdrop against which the drama of Tennessee and his partner unfolds. It is this blend of historical authenticity and emotional universality that makes *Tennessee's Partner* such a compelling and enduring piece of American literature.

Tennessee's Partner

I don't believe we ever learned his actual name. Our lack of knowledge about it never caused us any social problems, because in Sandy Bar in 1854, most men received new names. Sometimes these nicknames came from distinctive clothing, like "Dungaree Jack," or from particular habits, as seen with "Saleratus Bill," who got his name from using too much of that chemical compound in his daily bread, or from an unfortunate mistake, as demonstrated by "The Iron Pirate," a gentle, harmless man who earned that ominous nickname through his unfortunate mispronunciation of "iron pyrites." This might have been the start of a crude system of naming, but I'm inclined to believe it happened because a man's real name back then depended entirely on his own word. "You call yourself Clifford, do you?" Boston said to a nervous newcomer with complete contempt. "Hell is packed with men like that!" He then introduced the poor fellow, whose name actually was Clifford, as "Jaybird Charley"—a spontaneous burst of inspiration that stuck with him forever.

But to return to Tennessee's Partner, whom we never knew by any other name than this family-related title; we only discovered later that he had once existed as his own separate and individual person. It appears that in 1853 he left Poker Flat to travel to San Francisco, supposedly to find himself a wife. He never made it any further than Stockton. In that town he became interested in a young woman who served tables at the hotel where he ate his meals. One morning he said something to her that made her smile in a not unfriendly way, playfully break a plate of toast over his upturned, earnest, innocent face, and then run back to the kitchen. He went after her, and came out a few minutes later, covered with even more toast but victorious. A week later they were married by a Justice of the Peace, and they returned to Poker Flat. I realize that this story could be told with more drama, but I choose to tell it the way it was told around Sandy Bar—in the mining camps and saloons— where all romantic feelings were tempered by a strong sense of humor.

Very little is known about their married happiness, possibly because Tennessee, who was living with his partner at the time, one day decided to say something to the bride on his own behalf. It's said that she smiled at him kindly and modestly withdrew, this time traveling as far as Marysville, where Tennessee followed her, and where they began living together without the help of a Justice of the Peace. Tennessee's Partner accepted the loss of his wife in a simple and serious manner, which was typical of his character. But to everyone's surprise, when Tennessee returned one day from Marysville without his partner's wife—she having smiled and left with someone else—Tennessee's Partner was the first man to shake his hand and greet him warmly. The men who had gathered in the canyon expecting to see a fight were naturally outraged. Their anger might have expressed itself through mockery, but there was a certain look in Tennessee's Partner's eye that showed he wouldn't appreciate any humor about the situation. Indeed, he was a serious man, with a steady focus on practical matters that made him unpleasant to deal with during conflicts.

Meanwhile a popular feeling against Tennessee had grown up among the lawyers. He was known to be a gambler; he was suspected to be a thief. In these suspicions Tennessee's Partner was equally implicated; his continued friendship with Tennessee after the incident mentioned above could only be explained by the theory that they were partners in crime. At last Tennessee's guilt became obvious. One day he caught up with a stranger on his way to Red Dog. The stranger later told that Tennessee entertained him with interesting stories and memories, but illogically ended the conversation with the following words: "And now, young man, I'll trouble you for your knife, your pistols, and your money. You see your weapons might get you into trouble at Red Dog, and your money's a temptation to those with bad intentions. I think you said your address was San Francisco. I shall try to visit." It should be mentioned here that Tennessee had a wonderful sense of humor, which no business concerns could completely suppress.

This exploit was his last. Red Dog and Sandy Bar joined forces against the highwayman. Tennessee was hunted in much the same way as his namesake, the grizzly bear. As the trap tightened around him, he made a desperate break through the Bar, firing his revolver at the crowd gathered in front of the Arcade Saloon, then continued up Grizzly Canyon; but at the far end he was blocked by a small man on a gray horse. The two men stared at each other for a moment in silence. Both were brave, both calm and self-reliant, and both represented a type of civilization that would have been called heroic in the seventeenth century, but in the nineteenth was simply termed "reckless." "What have you got there?—I call," said Tennessee quietly. "Two bowers and an ace," replied the stranger just as calmly, revealing two revolvers and a bowie knife. "That beats me," Tennessee responded; and, with this gambler's saying, he tossed aside his empty pistol and rode back with his captor.

It was a warm night. The cool breeze that typically arose when the sun set behind the chaparral-covered mountain was absent from Sandy Bar that evening. The small canyon was suffocating with hot, resinous smells, and the rotting driftwood on the Bar released faint, nauseating fumes. The day's feverish heat and intense emotions still permeated the camp. Lights moved restlessly along the riverbank, casting no reflection in its muddy waters. Against the dark backdrop of the pine trees, the windows of the old loft above the express office glowed starkly bright; and through their bare panes, the people gathered below could see the silhouettes of those who were at that very moment determining Tennessee's fate. And above all of this, outlined against the dark sky, the Sierra mountains rose up, distant and emotionless, topped with even more distant and emotionless stars.

Tennessee's trial was conducted as fairly as possible, given that the judge and jury felt somewhat obligated to justify their verdict based on the earlier irregular arrest and charges. Sandy Bar's justice system was unforgiving but not driven by revenge. The excitement and personal emotions from the chase had subsided; now that they had Tennessee safely in custody, they were prepared to listen patiently to any defense, though they were already convinced it would be inadequate. Since they had no doubt in their minds about the outcome, they were willing to give the prisoner the benefit of any uncertainty that might exist. Confident in their belief that he deserved to be hanged on general principles, they allowed him more freedom in his defense than his reckless boldness seemed to warrant. The Judge appeared more worried than the prisoner, who seemed otherwise unbothered and clearly took dark satisfaction in the situation he had caused. "I'm not playing any part in this game," had been his consistent but good-natured response to every question. The Judge—who had also captured him—briefly and vaguely wished he had shot him on sight that morning, but quickly dismissed this human weakness as beneath the dignity of judicial thinking. However, when someone knocked at the door and announced that Tennessee's Partner was there to speak for the prisoner, he was immediately admitted without hesitation. Perhaps the younger jury members, who were finding the proceedings tediously serious, welcomed him as a welcome distraction.

He certainly wasn't an impressive-looking man. Short and heavy-set, with a square face burned by the sun to an unnaturally deep red color, dressed in a loose canvas work shirt and pants stained and spattered with red dirt, he would have looked odd under any circumstances, and now appeared downright comical. When he bent down to set a heavy carpet bag at his feet, it became clear from the partially visible writing and designs that the fabric used to patch his pants had originally been meant for something far less practical. Still, he approached with great seriousness, and after shaking hands with each person in the room with deliberate friendliness, he wiped his solemn, troubled face with a red bandanna handkerchief that was slightly lighter than his skin tone, placed his strong hand on the table to support himself, and spoke to the Judge: "I was passing by," he started, as if apologizing, "and I thought I'd just drop in and see how things were going with Tennessee there—my partner. It's a hot night. I can't remember weather like this before on the Bar."

He stopped for a moment, but since no one else offered any weather-related memories, he reached for his handkerchief again and spent several moments carefully wiping his face.

"Do you have anything to say on behalf of the prisoner?" the Judge asked finally.

"That's it," said Tennessee's Partner, in a tone of relief. "I came here as Tennessee's partner, having known him for nearly four years, on and off, through good times and bad, in luck and out of luck. His ways aren't always my ways, but there isn't anything about that young man, there isn't any mischief he's been up to, that I don't know about. And you say to me, you say—confidentially, and between man and man—you say, 'Do you know anything in his favor?' and I say to you, I say—confidentially, as between man and man—'What should a man know about his partner?'"

"Is this all you have to say?" the Judge asked impatiently, sensing that a risky shared sense of humor was starting to make the courtroom feel more human.

"That's right," Tennessee's Partner went on. "It's not my place to say anything against him. So what's the situation here? Tennessee needs money, needs it badly, and doesn't want to ask his old partner for it. So what does Tennessee do? He waits for a stranger and catches that stranger; then you wait for him and catch him; and it all evens out. And I'm asking you, being a fair-minded man, and all of you gentlemen, as fair-minded men, if this isn't exactly how it happened."

"Prisoner," the Judge said, cutting him off, "do you have any questions for this man?"

"No! No!" Tennessee's Partner continued urgently. "I'm handling this situation by myself. To get straight to the point, it's simply this: Tennessee here has behaved pretty badly and cost a stranger and this camp a lot of trouble. So now, what's the right thing to do? Some people would say more is needed; others would say less. Here's seventeen hundred dollars in raw gold and a watch—it's basically everything I own—and let's call it even!" And before anyone could move to stop him, he had dumped everything from the carpet bag onto the table.

For a moment his life hung in the balance. One or two men jumped to their feet, several hands reached for concealed weapons, and a proposal to "throw him from the window" was only prevented by a gesture from the Judge. Tennessee laughed. And seemingly unaware of the commotion, Tennessee's Partner took advantage of the moment to wipe his face again with his handkerchief.

When order was restored, and the man was made to understand through forceful language and persuasion that Tennessee's crime could not be forgiven with money, his face took on a more serious and threatening expression, and those who were closest to him noticed that his rough hand trembled slightly on the table. He paused for a moment as he slowly put the gold back into the carpetbag, as if he had not yet fully grasped the high sense of justice that guided the court, and was confused by the thought that he had not offered enough. Then he turned to the Judge, and saying, "This here is a lone hand, played alone, and without my partner," he bowed to the jury and was about to leave, when the Judge called him back. "If you have anything to say to Tennessee, you had better say it now." For the first time that evening the eyes of the prisoner and his strange defender met. Tennessee smiled, showed his white teeth, and saying, "Beaten, old man!" held out his hand. Tennessee's Partner took it in his own, and saying, "I just stopped by as I was passing to see how things were going," let the hand fall limply, and adding that "it was a warm night," mopped his face again with his handkerchief, and without another word left.

The two men never saw each other alive again. The unprecedented insult of attempting to bribe Judge Lynch—

who, regardless of being prejudiced, weak, or close-minded, was absolutely honest—solidified in that legendary figure's mind any uncertain decision about Tennessee's destiny; and at dawn he was escorted, under heavy guard, to face his fate at the summit of Marley's Hill.

How he faced it, how calm he remained, how he refused to speak, how flawless the committee's preparations were— all of this was thoroughly documented in the Red Dog Clarion by its editor, who witnessed the event firsthand, along with a cautionary moral lesson and warning to all future wrongdoers, and I gladly direct readers to his powerful prose. However, the splendor of that midsummer morning, the perfect harmony between earth, air, and sky, the vibrant life stirring in the untamed woods and hills, nature's joyful rebirth and promise, and most importantly, the boundless peace that pulsed through everything, went unreported, since it wasn't considered part of the social instruction. Yet when the pathetic and senseless act was completed, and a life, with all its potential and obligations, had departed from the twisted form that swayed between earth and sky, the birds continued singing, the flowers kept blooming, the sun kept shining just as brightly as before; and perhaps the Red Dog Clarion was correct.

Tennessee's Partner wasn't among the group that had gathered around the threatening tree. But as they began to scatter, their attention was caught by the strange sight of a motionless donkey-cart stopped beside the road. When they came closer, they immediately recognized the old Jenny and the two-wheeled cart as belonging to Tennessee's Partner— he used them to haul dirt from his mining claim. A short distance away sat the owner of this equipment himself, positioned under a buckeye tree and wiping sweat from his flushed face. When someone asked him what he was doing there, he explained that he had come for the body of the "deceased," "if it was acceptable to the committee." He didn't want to "rush anything"; he could wait. He wasn't working that day, and once the gentlemen had finished with the "deceased," he would take him away. "If there's anyone here," he continued in his straightforward, earnest manner, "who would like to join the funeral, they're welcome to come." Maybe it was due to the sense of humor that I've already mentioned was characteristic of Sandy Bar—or perhaps it stemmed from something even finer than that—but two-thirds of the bystanders immediately accepted his invitation.

It was noon when Tennessee's body was delivered into the hands of his partner. As the cart pulled up to the fatal tree, we saw that it held a rough rectangular box—apparently constructed from a piece of sluicing equipment—and half filled with bark and pine tassels. The cart was also decorated with willow branches and made fragrant with buckeye blossoms. When the body was placed in the box, Tennessee's Partner pulled a piece of tarred canvas over it and solemnly climbed onto the narrow seat in front, placing his feet on the shafts as he urged the little donkey forward. The vehicle moved slowly ahead at that dignified pace that was typical of Jenny even under less serious circumstances. The men—some curious, some joking, but all good-natured—walked alongside the cart; some ahead, some trailing behind the simple funeral procession. However, whether due to the narrowing road or some instinctive sense of propriety, as the cart continued forward, the group fell back in pairs, marching in step and taking on the appearance of a formal procession. Jack Folinsbee, who had initially performed a silent funeral march on an imaginary trombone, stopped his performance due to lack of sympathy and appreciation—not possessing, perhaps, the true comedian's ability to be satisfied with enjoying his own humor.

The path wound through Grizzly Canyon, now draped in somber shadows and darkness. The towering redwoods, their roots buried deep in the red earth, stood in a single line along the trail, their drooping branches seeming to offer a rough blessing to the funeral procession passing below. A rabbit, startled into frozen stillness, sat upright and trembling among the roadside ferns as the mourners walked by. Squirrels scrambled up to higher branches to get a better view, while blue jays spread their wings and fluttered ahead of the group like escorts, continuing until they reached the edge of Sandy Bar and the isolated cabin where Tennessee's Partner lived.

Even under better conditions, this wouldn't have been a pleasant location. The unattractive setting, the crude and ugly structures, and the unpleasant features that marked the settlements built by California miners were all present here, made even worse by the gloom of abandonment. A short distance from the cabin stood a rough fence that had once enclosed a garden during the brief period when Tennessee's Partner had been happily married, but now wild ferns had taken over completely. As we walked closer, we were shocked to discover that what we had mistaken for a recent gardening effort was actually disturbed earth surrounding an open grave.

The cart stopped in front of the fenced area, and with the same quiet confidence he had shown all along, Tennessee's Partner turned down any help that was offered. He hoisted the crude coffin onto his back and placed it into the shallow grave all by himself. After that, he hammered down the wooden board that acted as a cover, then climbed up onto the small pile of dirt next to the grave, removed his hat, and carefully wiped his face with his handkerchief. The gathered crowd sensed this was leading up to him saying something, so they found spots to sit on tree stumps and rocks, waiting to hear what he would say.

"When a man," Tennessee's Partner began slowly, "has been running free all day, what's the natural thing for him to do? Why, to come home. And if he's not in any condition to go home, what can his best friend do? Why, bring him home! And here's Tennessee who has been running free, and we bring him home from his wandering." He paused and picked up a piece of quartz, rubbed it thoughtfully on his sleeve, and continued: "This isn't the first time that I've carried him on my back, as you saw me now. This isn't the first time that I brought him to this cabin when he couldn't help himself; this isn't the first time that Jinny and I have waited for him on that hill, and picked him up and brought him home like this, when he couldn't speak and didn't recognize me. And now that it's the last time, well"—he paused and rubbed the quartz gently on his sleeve— "you can see it's pretty hard on his partner. And now, gentlemen," he added suddenly, picking up his long-handled shovel, "the funeral's over; and my thanks, and Tennessee's thanks, to you for your trouble."

Refusing any offers of help, he started filling in the grave, turning his back on the crowd, which, after hesitating for a few moments, slowly walked away. As they crossed the small ridge that blocked Sandy Bar from sight, some people, glancing back, believed they could see Tennessee's Partner, his task completed, sitting on the grave with his shovel resting between his knees and his face buried in his red bandanna handkerchief. However, others argued that you couldn't distinguish his face from his handkerchief at such a distance; and this matter remained unsettled.

In the aftermath that followed the intense excitement of that day, Tennessee's Partner wasn't overlooked. A private investigation had cleared him of any involvement in Tennessee's wrongdoing, leaving behind only questions about his mental state. Sandy Bar made it a priority to visit him and offer various crude but sincere acts of kindness. However, from that day forward, his robust health and considerable strength appeared to visibly deteriorate; and when the rainy season truly began, and the small blades of grass started to emerge from the rocky hill above Tennessee's grave, he became bedridden.

One night, when the pine trees beside the cabin swayed in the storm and dragged their thin branches across the roof, and the roar and rush of the swollen river could be heard below, Tennessee's Partner raised his head from the pillow, saying, "It's time to go get Tennessee; I need to hitch Jinny to the cart," and he would have gotten up from his bed if not for his caretaker holding him back. Fighting against the restraint, he continued with his strange delusion: "There, now, steady, Jinny—steady, old girl. How dark it is! Watch out for the ruts—and watch out for him too, old gal. Sometimes, you know, when he's completely drunk, he falls down right in the middle of the path. Keep going straight up to the pine tree on top of the hill. There! I told you so!— there he is—coming this way too—all by himself, sober, and his face glowing. Tennessee! Partner!"

And so they met.

Here ends Number Three of the western classics, Being Tennessee's Partner by Bret Harte, with an introduction by William Dallam Armes. The photogravure frontispiece was created by Albertine Randall Wheelan. Of this First Edition, One Thousand Copies have been published, printed on Fabriano handmade paper. The typography was designed by J. H. Nash. Published by Paul Elder and Company, and produced as a book for them at the Tomoye Press, New York City, in the year Nineteen Hundred and Seven.

THE END

Thank You For Reading

You've Just Read a Piece of the Greatest Library Ever Rebuilt

Thank you for reading.

This book is one of thousands we're restoring, reimagining, and translating as part of the **Modern Library of Alexandria** — a global movement to preserve and share humanity's most important ideas.

What was once lost to fire and time is now rising again — not just as memory, but as living, breathing knowledge, freely accessible to all.

What You Can Do Next:

- **Keep Reading.**

  Discover more legendary works — in beautiful print, audiobook, or digital form — at LibraryofAlexandria.com.

- **Build Your Own Library.**

  Every title is available as a paperback, hardcover, or collectible boxset — at true printing cost. Craft a personal library worthy of display.

- **Spread the Light.**

  Share this book. Tell others about the movement. Help us translate every timeless work into every language, so no reader is ever left behind.

By finishing this book, you've already taken part in something extraordinary.

Join us at LibraryofAlexandria.com

Together, we're rebuilding the greatest library the world has ever known.

With appreciation,

The Modern Library of Alexandria Team

Visit:
www.libraryofalexandria.com
Or scan the code below:

www.ingramcontent.com/pod-product-compliance
Lightning Source LLC
Chambersburg PA
CBHW012205030726
47494CB00022B/2372